WAY OF LIGHT

WAY OF LIGHT

Cedric Paul Harriott as Abbot Kai Kihran

2016

Copyright © 2016 by Master Mystic Monk Heh Heru

All rights reserved. This book or any portion thereof may not be reproduced or used in any manner whatsoever without the express written permission of the publisher except for the use of brief quotations in a book review or scholarly journal.

First Printing: 2017
Third Edition

ISBN 978-1-951881-02-3

Cultured Melanin Literary & Visual Arts Studios
44 Shipping Place
PO Box #4042
Baltimore, MD 21222

https://www.culturedmelanin.studio

Introduction: Way of Light

The Way of Light is a philosophy for the way of living peacefully, prosperously, and purposefully; without the fear matrix and it is a philosophy that exudes itself in the mastery of peace, love, harmony, empathy, knowledge, mysticism, balance, and self-defense of the peace state.

It incorporates the attributes of the intentionality of actions, compassion-centered living, mindfulness of the whole & all of its sub-parts, master student focus point, a more natural balance of push and pull, as well as an overall rejuvenation of the modern mystic monk style of living. It is also a way that does not mask the lower natures of humans, and it does not seek to separate itself from the ills of humankind. It is a way that showcases how we should manage our responses in all of our affairs. This way does not pretend that if we are at peace and open to love that all will be well; this is equally a way of love and defense from a peace-centered state.

This work is for the general traveler that is not a traveler of our mystic rites but rather is on a solo journey of self-discovery, self-healing, self-actualization, and self-care. We do not submit that anyone who seeks the Way of Light should be held in destitution from this work and so we release it to all of our fellow travelers on this Spaceship Earth.

This work is a collection of the pearls of wisdom, sayings, quotes, and passages written or spoken from our mystery school & monk monastery founder, Master Mystic Monk Heh Heru unless otherwise noted. It is filled with his simple yet profound sensibilities, philosophies, and overall ways of being.

To further illustrate the Way of Light's methodology our founder, through our Mystic Degrees Programs, wrote:

"Some people experience the Sunrise in the morning and think nothing of it aside from the observation that they enjoy it so; continuing their day onward to the local coffee shop for an espresso or to the theater to see the new summer box office hit film on whatever the entertainment news told them to check out.

And...

Some people experience the Sun in its many stages and ask themselves: Why is it here? What are you? Where did it come from? What governs the nature of the elements that cause it to shine? What exactly is the sensation known as "warm"? How many other "Sun stars" are in the universe? Just how expansive is the universe? What is the nature of gravity and magnetics as it relates to the Sun, to the Earth, and to our physical form as Humans? Who am I? Where did I come from? Why do I wonder so intensely on the nature of the world around me and within me? Why am I so unfulfilled without these answers?"

The travelers seeking the path of the Second Sun observer are those in perfect form to receive this art while those who are of the first Sun observer will also find great beauty in the Way of Light if they so allow it to occur.

In our monk monastery and mystery school we are taught by our founder that we should "Seek the answers; enjoy the journey" and that we should "Always realize that we will never be more than master students here; in this space, we always leave room to grow."

Take from these lessons the gift of mindfulness as you progress through whatever life matrix you currently reside within. Let this be a working foundation to unlocking the Way of Light to the Guru within all of you.

We hope you enjoy the Way of Light or in the Kemetic Medu Neter language, Meten iny Sasap. And we hope that it delivers to you what we founded our school in search of increasing; the Guru within you.

WAY OF LIGHT

Way of Light: **TRUST**

Trust is the one bond of the social contract that can fall apart with more of a grandiose vaporization than the particles within a supernova, or it may bind things together as closely and intensely as the carbon particles that fuse together to manifest diamonds; the way the Earthen folds is entirely based upon your intentions and subsequent actions. A mage of the Way of Light seeks never to violate or break the trust bond.

– TRUST (Mystics Version)

Way of Light: **TRUST**

Trust is the one bond of our social interactions that could break apart like a toothpick in the hands of a Giant or grow as strong as the Great Redwood trees of California and resist being befallen by a lumberjack as if he were yielding a plastic spoon. The place you find yourself is solely based on your intentionality of action & thought. Don't break trust.

– **TRUST (Commons Version)**

Way of Light: **APPRECIATION**

Don't fall. But if you do then enjoy the view; just don't stay there too long. In all, there is a message. Listen to her for she is the brightest star in the all.

– APPRECIATION

Way of Light: **MORALITY**

Why be good? Because, why be bad?

What benefit to our spiritual state rises form the evil natures of being? None, if you are of the Way of Light.

– MORALITY

Way of Light: **INTRAPERSONAL**

What is the purpose of who you are? The spark of the hidden one that animates your reality is a known enigma. Find meaning in your suffrages and then observe their purpose.

– INTRAPERSONAL (Mystics Version)

Way of Light: **PURPOSE**

To every action, there should be a gain. If not, everything remains in stagnation.

– **PURPOSE** *from* **Ur-Atum Rashidi Re**

Way of Light: **BUILDING**

The wise listens to the folly but succumbs not to their matrix.

– **BUILDING**

Way of Light: **IMPORTANCE**

Gold has value only because you so deem it to have it. Gold is as intrinsically worthless as diamonds to a person starved of food, water, and shelter.

– **IMPORTANCE**

Way of Light: **KNOWLEDGE**

The moment you submit to the cessation of knowledge is the moment you have become spiritually, physically, emotionally, and metaphorically dead.

– KNOWLEDGE

Way of Light: **RECIPROCITY**

Why harm the fly?
Just because it annoys you?
Because you can?
Leave it be.

– **RECIPROCITY**

Way of Light: **LONGEVITY**

Live in the moment…
The moment that never stops.

– LONGEVITY

Way of Light: **HONESTY**

You say you seek the truth but how often do you lie?

– **HONESTY**

Way of Light: **HONOR**

Honor is an ironic one. It's relative. What is honorable to one is an atrocity to another. Even in the Common Good this article can become easily corrupted by societal whims in improper form. On guard for this harm, for this is no place for a master mystic monk of our mystic rites. Always seek to align honor with the most just common good principle of doing no harm.

– HONOR

Way of Light: **VEGANISM**

Being a vegan means to resolve oneself with compassion continually. Being a non-vegan, aware of the truth of sentience is simply ignoring this because one wishes to harm animals and the Earth for selfish desires. Therefore, a master mystic monk of our mystic rites resolves with the lifestyle of veganism for this life and the next.

– VEGANISM

Way of Light: **WASTE**

Simply do not waste. Simply do not resolve in excess. Use what is needed within reasonable means from a compassion-centered perspective. What good is a five-course meal to me when my neighbor is starved and what good is four acres of land for the use of one single and solo man? Share the wealth or enjoy the folly nature of selfish desires, the choice is yours.

– WASTE

Way of Light: **FOCUS**

When at work, work.
When at rest, rest.
When at play, play.
In all be with focus on the task at hand.

– FOCUS

Way of Light: **PERSPECTIVE**

The bull is not naturally upset, the snake is not naturally enraged, and the turtle not naturally fearful. We learn from our environment with the baseline being our DNA bred instincts. See things differently and have caution not to overly categorize or mis-categorize for this is the folly's amusement park.

– PERSPECTIVE

Way of Light: **RELATIONAL**

The Sun does not shine for itself or by itself, and the leaves do not grow for themselves or by themselves. The nature of things is to share without causing harm to oneself. Be in that form for that is the revelation.

– **RELATIONAL**

Way of Light: **SELF-CARE**

What you eat is you.
What you drink is you.
What you breathe is you.
What you wear is you.
Biochemically speaking, whatever is within reach of you becomes of you. It is complicated but simple; present and yet ignored.

– SELF-CARE

Way of Light: **ANGER**

Live in anger if you wish; the volcano eventually implodes within itself.

Live in anger if you wish; the earthquake eventually subsides, and life goes on.

Live in anger if you wish; it will only hurt you and life still, will continue.

– ANGER

Way of Light: **BALANCE**

In the bitter uncomforting of the situations, we sometimes find ourselves within, calm breathing, constant prosperous activity, and the mourning over what saddens you are all equally important. Equally, too much of anything becomes poisonous.

– **BALANCE (Commons Version)**

Way of Light: **SILENCE**

Playing "rests" are oftentimes the best parts of a musical composition. In those spaces, you're neither speaking outward towards something or listening to something of the same but rather… you are simply in the subtext… chillin'

– SILENCE

Way of Light: **LOVE**

Love requires very strict rules and laws, all of which are unconditional. The law of trust, the law of transparency, the law of authenticity, the law of communication, the law of clarity, the law of intention, and the law of reciprocity. These are the cores. If you aren't willing to submit to them completely, then you don't know what love is.

– LOVE

Way of Light: **TERRA**

You are the spider in another life convergence, would you like to be squashed or feared for merely existing? No. Then act like you innerstand that we are all connected on this spiritual level and give no credence to the will of fear or its best friend misunderstanding.

– TERRA

Way of Light: **LOVE**

To love is your weakness; vulnerable you are bare. But is it worth the risks?

– LOVE

Way of Light: **RELATIONSHIPS**

Show me your demons.

Let us rob them of their sanctity together.

I am not scared to know all of you.

And I promise not to leave you to deal alone.

WE got this.

I knew what I signed up for when I first dropped the "I Love You" bomb.

Let us get this work done.

– RELATIONSHIPS

Way of Light: **LOVE**

I'm the one that won't abandon you just because the road conditions become as uncomfortable and dangerous as the ocean is deep. Your pain becomes "ours," and you baggage becomes "ours" for that is the truth of my love.

If you got paralyzed and I had to clean you up after you utilized the restroom I'd do it faster than the space between a hearts beat.

If you gained one hundred pounds or lost one hundred pounds, I'd still hold you with the same passion that a mother holds her newborn or a good father protecting his family.

I'll love you past the hardened days because I love hard, deeply, and always.

– LOVE

Way of Light: **HONOR**

Many will want you. But few will invest in you.

Many times people will "want" you; your body, your temporary energy, your anti-loneliness attention, or other temporary and fleeting areas but only a few people will invest in you – getting to know all of you, getting comfortable with all of you, investing themselves into your dreams, your visions, your passions – only a few people will drive five hours to see you for one. Only a few will do the most to create the conditions for new and beautiful experiences. Only a few will quite literally die for you if it came down to it.

Value those connections with a particular care for those are the foundations built on bedrock squared & a thousand and one times tenfold.

– HONOR

Way of Light: **HONESTY**

A lie can tear asunder everything that was once on hallowed ground.

Trust is one of the greatest factors within any bond. Trust can be withered away by the lack of communication, by the lack of transparency, by the lack of honesty, by the lack of authenticity, and by the lack of respect. Do not fall here. For to fall here is not of the Way of Light.

– HONESTY

Way of Light: **PRIORITY**

How many people claim that they're "too busy" these days? Everyone has time to themselves to eat, sleep, relax, or whatever else they wish to do. Everyone, equally, has time to make conversation with someone they care about. We make time for what we want to make time for and let no excuse ruin this revelation.

– PRIORITY

Way of Light: **FORM**

Nothing is solid; everything is energy.
Nothing is at rest; everything is in motion.
Nothing is hidden; everything is effortlessly present.
Nothing is dangerous; everything is perilous.
Nothing is safe; everything is unassailable.
Nothing has changed but change itself.
These are the revelation.

– FORM (Mystics Version)

Way of Light: **FORM**

Seek not the wind but rather sit at the mountain's summit where the wind flows uninterrupted; be in proper form to receive the art.

– FORM (Commons Version)

Way of Light: **CHOICES**

Making choices is something that governs all beings regardless of the species. From the nimble ant to the giant elephant, all of what occurs within us and around us is a result of our decisions. They often will have far reaching consequences beyond what we may immediately see; for some living in the moment is the path, for others watching the bigger picture is the path. In either case being aware of yourself and the choices you make is vital for life balance & essential for growth.

– **CHOICES (Mystics Version)**

Way of Light: **CHOICES**

Choices should be made from: clarity of thought, expressed intent, transparency of mind, an authenticity of heart, and concrete resolve; from these places, you need to own it wholly.

– **CHOICES (Commons Version)**

Way of Light: **INTRAPERSONAL**

Search for the "I" within.

– **INTRAPERSONAL** (Commons Version)
from **Ur-Atum Rashidi Re**

Way of Light: **DECEPTION**

The benefits of deception are for the deceptor the negative fortune of deception is for the deceived. If you would not appreciate the negative fortune of deception placed upon you or yours, then it is not in proper form to accept the benefits of being the deceptor.

– **DECEPTION (Commons Versions)**

Way of Light: **BLOCKAGE**

A blockage in your journey is part of your path. Don't look at an obstruction as a mechanism of defeat but rather as an opportunity to grow and learn new skills, powers, & efficiencies.

– BLOCKAGE

Way of Light: **LOSS**

How we deal with loss is a defining portion of how we are managing our emotional state. Almost no other state aside from rage, anger, and pain can so easily be over-lasting. We must make certain that we keep in our mind's eye the realization that all loss is relative and that we should not reside within its realm for too long; we should instead "feel" the emotion, and soon after let it pass for this is the Way of Light.

– **LOSS**

Way of Light: **HARM**

Always seek to avoid self-harm and outward harm. But if one finds themselves in such a state, find meaning and lessons within this place and try harder to avoid this place again for harm is not in the interest of or the Way of Light.

Balance is essential yes, however, in this particular space the risk stemming from the consequences of harm are far too negative to hold any operative value; perceive the benefits from a speculative space whereby damage is not active but rather a teaching tool in the manifestation of your mind only.

– **HARM**

Way of Light: **FAILURE**

Failure is an integral part of the Way of Light and every other pathway as well. It is unavoidable, but it is also a sacred principle of balance. Find meaning in the failure, lessons in the defeat, and a plan of action to not repeat it so. This is the Way of Light. Realize that failure is a part of the experiential experience and flow with it all in proper form.

– **FAILURE (Commons Version One)**

Way of Light: **FAILURE**

Failure can break you like a bull expressing its rage through a fine China shop, or it can be learned from like preventing the bull from expressing its rage in your fine China shop a second time. Easily expressed, learn from the failure what to do and not to do in the forward for that is the Way of Light. Realize failure is a part of the path and should be valued but not overused.

– FAILURE (Commons Version Two)

Way of Light: **PROGRESSION**

Always grow. Always.

– **PROGRESSION (Commons Version)**

Way of Light: **DEFENSE**

Misplaced trust or love will sting as badly as a bus-sized Hornet piercing your skin; an emotionally fatal wound. Study the arts of non-verbal communication, psycho-spirituality, and the psychological characteristics of humans; guard yourself against the ill will and intent of those who are not wholly for you or do not know themselves enough and harm you in the same way. These will throw you off the Way of Light and cause upon you to potentially fall into lasting despair, depression, sadness, and anger. Be aware that not all is good – be at peace with this fact but safe in your application of defense.

– **DEFENSE**

Way of Light: **APPRECIATION**

You do not get to decide who cares for you. Observe who is honestly for you and treat them well for that is the Way of Light.

– APPRECIATION

Way of Light: **PEACE + DEFENSE**

Even in the middle of a hurricane the "eye" is always chill. Be the "eye" and use the power of the storm to defeat any threat against your peace-centered space for that is the Way of Light.

Easily expressed, the eye is your peace-centered state, and the storm winds are the defenses in proper form setup to repel any negative force from piercing its veil.

Be the Hurricane.

– PEACE & DEFENSE

Way of Light: **DOGMA**

Seek more light and wisdom from all sources of light. Just as the nations of the world are separated by ethnic grouping, creed, culture, and imaginary borders you must become translucent and transmute past the distractions of the experiential layer for this is the crown perception and in form with the Way of Light.

– **DOGMA (Mystics Version)**

Way of Light: **DOGMA**

Any doctrine that enforces its philosophy with violence and harm or the threat of violence and harm is not of the Way of Light; question any articles that claim to provide salvation upon submittal through violence. Read and study all materials and seek only the absolution of the truth for that is the Way of Light and an inherent quality in all of our Mystic Monks.

– **DOGMA (Commons Version)**

Way of Light: **PROGRESSION**

Seek the answers; enjoy the journey.

– PROGRESSION (Mystics Version)

Way of Light: **CONSUMERISM**

A diamond ring is a status of conspicuous consumption in its most current application. To a starving person, a diamond is nothing more than a pebble on the road. Conspicuous consumption is not the Way of Light. Do not acquire material things to show them off to others who are not of the same status but rather acquire material things to enhance the quality of the spiritual life around you with equal benefit to you and do not overconsume for the sake of consuming for this is the Way of Light.

If I purchase ten pounds of African Black Soap that expires in one week, I should give away nine pounds of it to others around me for it would be a waste for it to expire without good use. This is the material spiritual relationship that we should seek in our lives.

– CONSUMERISM

Way of Light: **JUSTICE + FORGIVENESS**

When someone wrongs you in any capacity, understand what drove their motivation but do not forgive them and do not forget the transgression. Be at peace with your own self enough to see the lesson in the situation and flow forward from there, but I believe it is folly and unwise to pretend that we should seek to forgive the transgression as if this is the Way of Light. The way of light is centered not only on our own individual inner peace but also the defense of our peace-centered state from any actor that seeks ill will towards it whether it be intentional or not, direct or indirect.

– JUSTICE & FORGIVENESS

Way of Light: **MORALITY**

Ethics and morals are relative to the lens one views life from. The Way of Light seeks to innerstand the ethics and morals of all parties of the world and to float the subtext between them to seek the best possible outcome for the Common Good and in doing no harm. It is a hard practice but worthy of practice the same.

– MORALITY

Way of Light: **BALANCE**

Correct yourself in the alignment with the divinity of the mystic's mind. Align yourself with the progression of the Way of Light always seeking the subtext connection. From this space between good and evil, right and left, forward and backward you find yourself "centered."

– **BALANCE (Mystics Version)**

Way of Light: **CAUTION**

The Way of Light is peace-centered, but it is also the defense of the peace-centeredness. Be cautious with who you allow to landscape the lands around your castle of defense for THAT is the Way of Light.

– CAUTION (Commons Version)

Way of Light: **CAUTION**

A speeding train cannot avoid a break in the railroad tracks; for it is progressing too fast to even see the flaw in the path. A respectable pace in due bounds with our ability to perceive the path is the only speed in which our train can see the break in the railroad tracks. The obvious choice is obvious to those who are of the Way of Light.

– **CAUTION (Mystics Version)**

Way of Light: **CYNICISM + LOVE**

Love is kind.
Love is key.
Love is hard.
Love hates me.
Love is patience.
Love is trust.
Love is vulnerable hidden by motives of our minds.
Love is peace.
Love is hope.
Love is strong; sometimes as strong as a broken rope.
Where love goes,
And what love is,
Love is guided by our motives, actions, and fears.

– CYNICISM & LOVE (Commons Version)

Way of Light: **JUST INTENTIONS**

How we treat others is truly a reflection of our character. If a person is just then they equally deserve just treatment, and the same action of thought goes towards those who are found unjust according to the common good of the Way of Light. That is to say, if the evil seeks your favor pay them no favor and if the just seeks your favor then pay them your favor for this is the nature of the Way of Light. It is truly all about intentions, so let them be just.

– JUST INTENTIONS (Mystics Version)

Way of Light: **JUST INTENTIONS**

How you see others is you.
How you treat others is you.
If I am just, treat me as so.
If I am unjust, treat me as so.
Be always, with the governance of the nature of the Way of Light's common good for this is the way of just intentions.

– JUST INTENTIONS (Commons Version)

Way of Light: **NIGHTMARE**

Do not ignore fear; the long and turbulent night.
Do not peacefully let it rage; the horrors around.
Do not give credence and validity to fear.

Know what fear is.
Know what is driving your fear.

Create the plan to mitigate it.
Create the plan to manage it.
Create the will always to maintain your plan.

Now revisit all of your nightmares point of inception.

– NIGHTMARE

Way of Light: **PERSISTENT FEAR**

Fear is a condition and a response, a trigger and a response. When it becomes unresolved for too long; persistent in nature – it is then that we must close ourselves to stimuli and address the fear, which is currently overburdening our balance. Address yourself, or it will cause you to harm others outside of yourself, and that is not the Way of Light.

– **PERSISTENT FEAR (Mystics Version)**

Way of Light: **PERSISTENT FEAR**

What scares us most will eventually consume us unless we quit running from the trigger and its inception point.

The rabbit can only run from the wolf for so long before it becomes too tired to fight back. Do not be folly and be the rabbit fighting the wolf away nay. Be the foods the wolf doesn't like, and be where the wolf is not comfortable; mitigate the fear and manage it accordingly for this is the Way of Light.

– PERSISTENT FEAR (Commons Version)

Way of Light: **FLEETINGNESS**

Many will claim to love you, only to show through actions that they don't.

Many will claim that you can trust them, only to show through actions that you cannot.

Many will claim that they are honest, only to show you that they only know lies.

Humans are as fleeting with their emotions and intentions as the universe is large. The key is to learn how to manage your response to their condition and how to see who they are before they even speak a word for this is the Way of Light.

– FLEETINGNESS

Way of Light: **TRAVELING**

The bug that spends its life in the jar is equally as much a slave as the human that spends their entire life void of worldly travels.

– **TRAVELING**

Way of Light: **VEGANISM**

Since we can live much healthier lives without harming animal friends and insect friends then why harm them at all? The choice is quite simple, either I enjoy harming animals because I desire their flesh in my mouth or I don't enjoy harming animals because they are not required for my physical growth or healthy for my spiritual body. The Way of Light is aligned forever with the ways of Veganism.

– VEGANISM

Way of Light: **AUTHENTICITY**

I am no different depending on the time of day.
I am who I showcase because why not be?

It requires too much energy and negative intentionality to be that which I am not naturally.

The tiger does not pretend to be the gorilla.
The tree does not pretend to be the butterfly.
The Earth does not pretend to be Mars.

We are who we are so why hide?
Behind makeup.
Behind fancy garments.
Behind false augmentations of beauty.
Behind obscure traditions such as heels or shaving.

As long as you are healthy, be happy.
As long as you are authentic, you're happy.

– **AUTHENTICITY (Mystics Version)**

Way of Light: **AUTHENTICITY**

I am not physically an ant so I won't pretend to be.

I am not a squirrel, so I won't pretend to be.

The tree is not a rock, and the rock is not a tree.

Be who you are, you'll find the "happy."

And.

You'll be free.

– AUTHENCITIY (Commons Version)

Way of Light: **TOLERANCE**

We all have tolerance innately within us, and it is in our best interest to learn to manage it as much as we do the relationships we allow around us.

The ant only tolerates a certain amount of noise and vibration around it before it flees, and the tree will only tolerate a certain temperature and humidity range before it responds to the stimuli.

We humans sometimes tolerate more than we should, and that only creates the antithesis of the Common Good.

If someone is hurting me, I will not have it around me. And if someone is placing negativity around me I will not stay. Knowing when to tolerate and when you've endured enough is a core of the defense area of the Way of Light. Master it as much as the dedication musician masters their craft.

– TOLERANCE

Way of Light: **KARMATIC PROVIDENCE**

Don't fear Karma but be aware that what you place outward into the path will eventually find its way to yours always.

Don't be good just out of fear of Karma's response.

Be good and righteous because of innerstanding that you should treat others the way you wish to be treated yourself; if I do not want to feel "harm", then I should not "harm" others unjustly.

Do this correctly, and Karma will be fair.
Ignore this and act unjustly and she will be just as fair.

– KARMATIC PROVIDENCE

Way of Light: **LIGHT + DARK**

Light is illumination, but only if darkness is the canvas.

Darkness is the whole for Light to shine the part.

Light is warmth, but only if darkness scales for the chill.

Darkness is the support for Light to take point.

The Way of Light is a path of self-leadership through the support of the whole of the universe, represented as darkness.

The Way of Light is a path that shares itself with the nature of Darkness; both are of the Common Good.

– LIGHT & DARK

Way of Light: **WATERS' WAY**

The nature of water is to flow everywhere no matter how slowly.

The nature of water does not mind if it must trickle with the speed of a raindrop in jar or crash like a wave into a jar of the same volume.

Water never seeks to be restricted or unrestricted; it just simply is what it is.

But even water has a law it must follow.

Nothing we see, touch, taste, feel, or hear is more than a rate of vibrations cast through the medium of the known enigma.

What governs the law of the nature of water?

What law governs that law?

Seek the answers; enjoy the journey.

This is the Way of Light.

– WATERS WAY

Way of Light: **SHALLOWNESS**

To be shallow is not at all within the Way of Light. If you seek physical depth in a pretty puddle instead of a deep ocean, then you are not of the Way of Light. Equally, if you physically, mentally, or spiritually shallow then you'll find nothing but disappointment in others and others will likely find absolutely nothing but disappointment in you. It's a whole backward world of imperfect perfections seeking their individual idea of perfect perfection; hopeless.

– SHALLOWNESS

Way of Light: **SHALLOW BEAUTY**

Pretty scent oils placed on odorous fecal matter doesn't change the fact that fecal matter is still going to be odorous.

Just because I place sewer water in a pretty glass bottle with fancy ornaments does not alter the fact that it is still sewer water.

Equally as true…

A pretty face is no cover for a horrible soul, with horrible character traits, and a horrible overall aura. Let us not be swayed by ill perceptions based on our lower natures for this is not the Way of Light. If you so enjoy shallow beauty then, by all means, eat the fecal matter and drink the sewer water anyway; that's your call completely.

– SHALLOW BEAUTY

Way of Light: **PSUEDOS' WAY**

Our path is not the only path; there are many.
From this you should find that we are master
students and fear not of any path for there is
always a possibility to find a jewel or two.
Any path that states it is the only say is, to me,
nothing more than the pseudos' way.

– PSUEDOS' WAY

Way of Light: **CONTENTION RESPONSE**

What good will come from the thought and action we manifest? This should be at the forefront of our minds always when we are in a social situation. Seeking always to de-escalate is the Way of Light. Stay in proper form, which is active listening, lasting composure, and with clear intentions; authentically.

We all have buttons don't let people push them if they do don't respond out of proper form. Find where others' buttons are and steer clear from pressing them unless it is just to do so for this is the Way of Light's principle on the protection of the peace-centered state.

– **CONTENTION RESPONSE (Mystics Version)**

Way of Light: **CONTENTION RESPONSE**

If you poke a bear with a needle how do you think it will respond? Easy... it will likely slash you in the face until you look like red oatmeal.

That needle is essentially pressing the bear's button. In following the Way of Light, the aggressor should never know what your reaction will be if pricked with a needle.

If I am pricked with a needle, my response will be based on lasting composure. What action comes from that should be a mystery to the aggressor.

This is the defense of the peace-centered state.

– **CONTENTION RESPONSE (Commons Version)**

Way of Light: **SELF-LIFE**

Work on self & exude peace.

– **SELF-LIFE**

Way of Light: **ACTIVE LISTENING**

Actively listen to the world.

Learn from all of the world without limitation.
All should be the teacher to my student.

– ACTIVE LISTENING

Way of Light: **JUDGEMENT**

No judgment; just flow.
Just be.
Just chill.

Be without judgment, just with peace & honor.

– JUDGEMENT

Way of Light: **THOUGHT RESPONSE**

Before you respond to stimuli ask yourself this question, "Is this where I want to be and who I want to be five minutes from now?" If you find your mind slipping into the ways of negative mental activity, the thought response should guide it from this place for it is a stress and depression mitigation tactic meant to defend the peace-centered state and this is the Way of Light.

– THOUGHT RESPONSE

Way of Light: **INNER LIGHT**

The Guru is naturally flowing within you, and through the application of proper form, this Guru becomes more available. The table for tea with the inner higher you is only available if you realize that no one is your leader or master but the "eye" within you and you subsequently master the connection to the Guru within you.

– INNER LIGHT (Mystics Version)

Way of Light: **INNER LIGHT**

The Guru is already within you. Whether they are healthy or not is dependent on whether or not you neglect them.

When you search for a leader outside of yourself and before yourself, you starve your Guru. When you submit to a religious system over all else and use that as a moral basis, you starve your Guru.

The connection pathway to the Guru within you is already within you. If it is in a dilapidated state or not is dependent on whether or not you neglect the upkeep of its way.

It is only when you work on the connection pathway within you and seek the leadership already within you that you blend with the inner light and that your Guru becomes available for tea time & wisdom building.

– **INNER LIGHT (Commons Version)**

Way of Light: **FLOW + LET GO**

Time will do what it does naturally, flow onward and always. You can ignore it like it doesn't exist and it will still do what it does naturally; go on. And you can watch it like a hawk does its prey and it will still do what it does naturally; go on. I love that lesson; just flow onward, always, and in proper form for that is the Way of Light.

– FLOW & LET GO

Way of Light: **TIME**

Time, or whatever you wish to call the forward progression of moments is and has always been.

What came first, the chicken or the egg? Easy, time. For without time the chicken and the egg are not relevant or manifested as a moment.

Time is the collection of moments passing.

Nothing matters without her law.

The Law of Time.

Flow through life unaffected, omnipresent, and powerful just like the Law of Time for that is the Way of Light.

– TIME

Way of Light: **EMOTIONS**

Emotions are a large part of our human condition; a powerful element of our overall health state. And as such it must be managed in proper form. How we allow ourselves to feel and what we project outward in response to what we feel defines not only our reality, but it also plays a part in governing how the world perceives us, how we perceive self, and what level of composure we have mastered. If someone makes you angry, you are faced with a choice to either respond in anger or to respond in a composed and calculated manner. If someone breaks your heart, you have a choice to either respond with sadness, depression, and anger or you can respond with a composed and calculated method. This isn't to say that you should sheath your emotions or fake them nay, rather play out the entire condition in your head by utilizing the "thought response" and other treasures of wisdom from the Way of Light. Master your emotional state and nay let it control you is the message and the Way of Light.

– EMOTIONS (Mystics Version)

Way of Light: **EMOTIONS**

You seek to anger me; I reroute the anger to the void.

You seek to sadden me; I encapsulate the sadness in my peace.

You seek to harm me; I reroute the harm to the void.

You seek to uplift me; I receive this, enhance this, and return it to you for this is the Way of Light.

Manage your emotions through the "thought response."

– **EMOTIONS (Commons Version)**

Way of Light: **HONORARY**

Honor your word with appropriate action.

If you say you love me, I demand you prove it in actions.

If you say you trust me, I demand you prove it in actions.

Honor is based on vulnerability + trust which are based on transparency, authenticity, and respect.

Honor yourself, and those who are just and worthy of being honored in return for this is the Way of Light.

– HONORARY

Way of Light: **STAMINA**

Peace is state that takes fortitude. It does not just arrive and stay out of providence. You must work diligently to always enhance your peace-centered state and to defend its place of residence. Only a weak tree will fall if accosted by an ants push. Be resolute and steadfast with the defense of your peace-centered state and have the stamina to stay the course no matter the conditions of the road for this is the Way of Light.

– STAMINA

Way of Light: **GRATEFUL**

Happy people that are grateful are great full people that are happy.

– **GRATEFUL** *from* **Tahirah Siti Ra**

Way of Light: **SELF-AWARENESS**

The path to the light of your awareness is your blueprint for life. It is a partway with many branches, twist, and turns meandering on a journey of self-discovery of your soul-personality.

– **SELF-AWARENESS** *from* **Ur-Atum Rashidi Re**

Way of Light: **TRUE LEARNING**

True learning is aggravating to the ignorance within you. Overcome that aggravation, and the Way of Light will be the reward.

— **TRUE LEARNING** *from* **Ur-Atum Rashidi Re**

Way of Light: **CLOSURE**

Closure is a dish best served organically.

– CLOSURE

www.ingramcontent.com/pod-product-compliance
Lightning Source LLC
Chambersburg PA
CBHW022013120526
44592CB00034B/797